www.finishinglinepress.com

HUMMING
AT THE DINNER TABLE

A Book of Poems

by

Joanne Esser

Finishing Line Press
Georgetown, Kentucky

HUMMING
AT THE DINNER TABLE

A Book of Poems

ACKNOWLEDGMENTS

Publisher: Leah Maines
Editor: Christen Kincaid
Cover Art: Wisconsin artist Carla Brown, carlabrownart.com.
Author Photo: Michael Gilligan, michaelgilliganphotography.com.
Cover Design: Elizabeth Maines McCleavy

Printed in the USA on acid-free paper.
Order online: www.finishinglinepress.com
                 also available on amazon.com

Author inquiries and mail orders:
Finishing Line Press
P. O. Box 1626
Georgetown, Kentucky 40324
U. S. A.

Table of Contents

ONE

"…Everything this well-guarded
remembers being soft once."

—Kelly Madigan,
from her poem "Porcupine"

MAKING THE BEDS

I can feel my mother's body best then:
wide hips, narrow hands,
her movements quick and sure.
Wrinkles in still-warm linens
I smooth and smooth again,
seeking a perfect surface, as she did.
My hands become hers.
I tuck corners square, fold back
just so much sheet over blankets,
spread the comforter, align its stripes,
fluff goose feathers with firm
shakes of the pillows. I do not sit
on the edge to put on my shoes;
I don't want to mess up
the straightness of my work.
I hear her voice in the whisper
of my hands sliding across sheets.

AFRICAN VIOLETS

She kept them in an iron stand in rows,
Pots of pinks and lavenders, shading all the way
To deepest purple, and always one pure white,
Near the one north-facing window in our house.
A bit exotic in a prim '60's rambler
Set in subdivision sprawl.

My mother's one diversion. How carefully
She watered them with her green tin watering can,
The exact amount required, not a drop more or less.
Luckily, it was her specialty, the dailyness of it,
And the pinching back.

Like a hoarded stash of something filched
From a land where she could never dream of going.
They smelled like soil and a dark secret must,
Leaves furred gray-green with dust, ancient things
That only thrived in slantwise light.

For a woman who dressed in beige,
Who let the gray sift through
Her hair, an odd delight. And the way
They kept on in spite of it, in the TV's
Constant flickering blue, the newspaper
Held up in front of his face,

Her attention to the ironing and mending,
Meat and potatoes on the table
Precisely at six. Those difficult flowers
At the edge of the room never faded,
Like a vision of a distant place
That she might somehow cultivate.

MATRIOSHKA

You open in the middle; little bodies emerge
from your big body: daughter from
mother, from grandmother,
from the first

mother. This is how you have always been.
So many layers to the center untwist
one by one until the tiniest doll,
almost too small to hold,
is released.

My daughter opens you, one wooden body
at a time, on the flowered rug.
As her small hands work,

she talks of her great-grandmother's
papery skin, her tired eyes, somehow
knowing her frail body lying
in a nursing home bed

is already hollow. "They will put her body
in a hole in the ground; they
will cover her with soil,"
my daughter says.

In her hands, your smallest halves open;
out pops your tiniest doll,
like a wooden seed.

My daughter scoops it up quick, remembers
to catch it before it is lost
in the thick carpet roses.

PORTRAIT WITH LIES

My father settles into smoke
at the end of each workday.
In his plaid, stiff-backed chair
he tells us tales of tall buildings
far beyond our window's reach,
peaks lost in a rainbowed sky.
My father drinks butterscotch rum
in a tall glass with ice
imported from bright islands where
no one like him would ever go.

My father sings with an open mouth
all the hymns his mother taught,
says Latin words he memorized,
Gloria Patri, et Filio…
when he was once an altar boy.
He bows down before the clock,
prays to keys and the television,
buries dollar bills in garden soil.
He flies to heaven on a plow
conjured from his boyhood farm.

He built our house of gray cement
without ornament or hinge,
sturdy when tornadoes blow.
My father goes to bed early,
though he says he never tires,
folds his hands upon his chest,
stares at stars straight through the roof.
When his dreams start tapping hard
on his forehead with demands,
he shoos them off like pesky flies.

PHOTO NEGATIVES

Remember the envelope in the back
of the black-and-white photo album,
the collection of negatives our mother
would never throw away?

How we used to hold the thin plastic
strips up to the light, see the world
made light, the light darkened,
everything familiar become strange.

Ghostly figures, shadows of people
we knew, smiling stiffly at the camera
as if from some alien place where
snow is black and trees glow luminous.

The flimsy transparency, bodies
we could almost see through,
standing on pale ground,
ominous skies pressing heavily down,

weighing on those people
from a simple day long ago
when our souls were nearly visible,
but only in retrospect.

On the day we were actually there,
the veil of the immediate clouded it all
with color, noise, the short-sighted
illusion of definition.

How easy it was then
in that mess of perception and youth
to believe that appearances
were the only true things.

DIGGING TO CHINA

Summer days we'd take our plastic shovels
and pails to the beach along Lake Michigan
to dig to the other side of the world.

We moved sand fast in serious heaps,
all our small muscles taut, piling
miniature mountains at the edge of the hole.

What if we really could break through
the center core that kept us from falling
to China, where people walk upside down?

We tested our power, arms in to the armpits,
chests laid out flat, our shovels bent
with the weight of dampening sand.

Then as far down as fingertips could go
a trickle of water began to flow
into the depths of our deepest place.

We jerked hands away, watched it stream in.
Hushed and excited, we didn't tell
the adults what we had managed to do:

dig all the way through the planet!
Now Chinese rivers would flood up from below
carrying people, all spun and confused

in a whirlpool of water that we had released,
cracking the world finally in half!
Our fearsome command over earth and sea

too much for us, we hurriedly scooped
handfuls of sand back into the hole,
to plug it up and stop the world's leak.

AUNTY FRITZ'S APARTMENT

You walk down the sidewalk with your mother
along the ivy-covered brick, push open
the heavy wooden door and run
through the darkened hallway that smells
of lilacs, old roses and dust
to the accordion gate, its brass criss-crosses
that squeeze together as you pull the handle across.

Step into the old elevator, push the button
that lifts you with a lurch, ascending
to your old great-aunty's home. Not a real
relative at all, not linked by blood but
by history, your mother's extra mother,
she is mythical and real at the same time.
It stops on the second floor. You slide the gate open

with a creak. The worn wool pattern of the carpet
leads you to her door. Your mother rings the bell,
but you know she will be expecting you,
sitting regal as a queen, curls of white hair
perfectly arranged, heavy jeweled earrings
weighing down her fleshy earlobes,
the faint scent in the air of Chanel No. 5,

settled in her ruby velvet chair as if
she has been there all day, just waiting
for you to arrive. Here is the china lamp
painted with flowers, the low cherry wood table,
its carved trim, the fringe along the bottom of the chair.
Things here are always in their places
on shelves, on the antique tiered table,

sparkle of detail on the decanter,
her single glass for brandy at bedtime.
You eye the cut-glass dish of butterscotch candies
wrapped in golden cellophane. You wait
until she says *Help yourself, my dear*,
and you take care to lift the glass lid
silently, with your utmost attention.

Everything here is old, and beautiful,
glinting in the polished afternoon sun,
like her. She has lived more years than anyone
you know, through untold loves and losses,
and beams the light of benevolence
beyond any circumstance, a gentle sweep
over the plush room, the smile of her

old blue eyes made larger through her thick lenses.
She laughs then, generous and genuine, amused
by your shyness. She calls you to her side.
You rise and tiptoe over, shift the glass cane
that hangs from the arm of her chair.
Her warm hands on your face like a blessing,
her touch reminds you how good you are.

FAMILY REUNION

I am trying hard not to get grass stains
on my Sunday dress as I fly across
my grandparents' perfect flat green lawn.
My fifteen cousins, whose names I still mix up
and am almost too shy to talk to, chase me
in Tag or Spud at the annual family reunion.

The garage has been swept, tools hung up
to make room for card tables, folding chairs,
big aluminum tubs of ice. We children wait
for permission to choose a soda: grape, cherry, orange
or my favorite, cream, and drink it, only today,
straight from the lips of the thick glass bottles.

The men sit with cigars, cards, bottles of beer.
Grandpa in a rocking chair listens to the ball game
blaring on a transistor radio. Six grown brothers barely talk.
Had they already said all they'll ever need to say
back in the days of their crowded farm house?
Their only sister's husband downs his sixth beer

and pulls out an accordion. Even I can hear the slur
of his words, see the disapproval of the brothers' crossed arms.
No one sings but Eddie, white hair like a wild Santa,
skinny legs in Bermuda shorts. I like the old-timey music
but won't say so, only tap my toes in rhythm quietly
until the aunts call me in to help in the kitchen,

the realm of the women. They arrange a tableful of dishes,
German potato salad, pork and beans, ham slices
and tiny buns for sandwiches, fancy Jello molds,
always one with fruit cocktail suspended in its redness.
Ladies' voices rise and swell like the chickens' squawking
on the old farm, news and gossip and how to arrange the food.

Grandma issues orders from her place next to the stove,
a tiny woman with rope-strong arms. She ties an old apron
over her home-sewn flower print housedress and uncovers
the three kuchens she has baked, as if she is again
feeding all the men come in from the fields
their big noon dinner. I do what she tells me to do.

When I'm supposed to call in the uncles and my boy cousins
from the yard, I don't want to, but I must, timid-voiced.
They line up in the kitchen, littlest children first, survey this spread of love
made visible without words, in the only way
this family knows how, and heap food on paper plates.
No one cares if we take more than one dessert.

Soon the women wash the dishes, men pack the coolers
into the trunks of the sedans. Someone steers Eddie to the
passenger side of his pick-up. I hear the aunts cluck their tongues
as his wife takes the car keys. The shakes of their heads say
He's never been one of us. The uncles shake hands, formally,
climb into the driver's seats. The aunts smile and wave.

Every Sunday afternoon my parents dutifully bring us
to visit my grandparents, to the quiet of their ranch house.
But we will not see the other relatives again
until that one day next August, and the August after that.
And after Grandma's and Grandpa's funerals, everyone scatters.
No more accordion music, no more games of Spud.
No one to tell me if I've got the story right.

DO-OVER

In kickball, it was what we did
When the ball skewed over the line
And an argument began
About whether it was *in* or *out.*

Another chance, given for free
So the kid who made the mistake,
The one close to tears or
On the verge of a screaming fit

Would have a way to carry on
For the sake of the game.
We bigger kids could grant
These bends in the rules

Because we owned them.
Such power! Such ultimate
Control for a short while over
This small bit of life.

Perhaps it was practice
For all the errors that we'd make
Later, the ones we now find
Impossible to fix.

Another word for grace.

STORIES TOLD IN BED

(after Robert Hass)

In the next subdivision there was a woods, she tells her husband, his
head settling in to the pillow, and when she was fourteen, she used to
walk barefoot on the melting tar road on long summer afternoons
alone, her feet toughened gray. The yards in the neighborhood smelled
of just-cut grass, humid greenness, bees at the clover. She'd cross
the busy street, go along Westwood toward the shady grove and find
this huge maple tree that had wide, low branches. She'd climb it
fast, with handholds and footholds she knew well. Once settled in its arms,
she'd begin to hum, softly at first, then louder. No one knew she was
there, in the midst of the dense leaves, looking out. No one in the world.

At the dinner table, her father would not permit her to hum. She wouldn't
even realize she was doing it until he frowned and reprimanded her
as he wolfed down his pot roast and baked potato. Her mother passed
the gravy. Her father liked the idea of a proper family dinner. So
she'd stop. But a little while later she'd forget, start humming mindlessly
until she saw her father's scowl, her mother's subtle shake of her head.

Now she sits up, pushes at the pillow behind her back, remembering
the tight lines around her mother's mouth, how she had studied them
when she was fourteen, how she'd wished many things were different.
Though he tries not to, her husband has begun to drowse, his eyes closing.
He rolls toward her, wraps his arm around her waist, already giving in
to dreams: tree branches, distant humming, the smell of just-cut grass.

CRESCENDO, PART TWO

At fifteen, I wrote
a poem about a dandelion
emerging from the ground—
or maybe from a crack
in the sidewalk, I can't
remember—the first
public revelation of my tender,
idealistic heart, in stark
black-and-white.
"*Crescendo*," I called it,
a word I admired
at the time, full of
heightened drama,
juxtaposed with the most ordinary
of flowers. Sister Jane
awarded my little poem
first prize in the literary magazine
at Divine Savior-Holy Angels
High School. Everyone got
a copy of the small, stapled booklet
with my name printed in it.
I was embarrassed to be
seen like that, my voice
made so visible, but also
secretly pleased—perhaps
how the dandelion felt,
at first, when it pushed up
into its crescendo.

WORK IS THE MEDICINE FOR DREAMS (*)

Seems like the silence in the house
might have gotten to be too much for her,
a strong and splitting force, but the rules were clear:
it was never to be mentioned.

Seems like my mother cleaned a lot,
scrubbing the bathroom until it shined,
dusting furniture, maybe thinking
a clean house could be worn like a badge
indicating her worthiness to an indifferent
world that never watched.

Seems like the photo I found in the very back
of her drawer tucked under silk scarves,
white gloves in slender boxes, next to the Mother's Day
scented dusting powder, a black-and-white photo
of her with a handsome man in a Navy uniform
who looked directly into her eyes
was saved for some true reason.

Seems like her choices were made too soon
and the silence slathered on like a cool salve
to close the wound might have trapped the hurt inside.
Seems like I should have figured it out a lot sooner.

(*) *The title is taken from Lucille Clifton's poem*
    "anna speaks of the childhood of mary her daughter"

TWO

"I call this song of needful love my voice."

—*Rafael Campo,*
from his poem "My Voice"

NEW LOVE

Even now
I remember it

the way the sun
striped the bed

how it wanted
to paint it yellow

how we sat in its
warm wanting

the way sunflowers
grow into light

their seedy faces
turned always toward it

their thick stems
holding solid

their ragged haloes
ringed in wanting

willing to wait
for that yellow

like us
on the bed

THE APPLE

He walks into the back garden of the old English hotel in early morning while she sips tea at the patio table. It is surprisingly warm and the dew sparkles on late summer flowers. It is the second morning of the brief time they will have here in this place of history and imagination. He disappears from view for a moment, then returns to her, walking back slowly. There is something in his hand, exactly the size of his cupped palm. He shows her: an apple. *It just fell into my hand when I reached up*, he insists. Deep red blush over shiny green skin, elegant unblemished roundness, they don't know what kind it is, but like a Dutch still life painted centuries ago, it glows in its gold-lit perfection. Then he takes a bite. He closes his eyes. Chews mindfully, extracting all the sensation from it. A drop of its juice at the corner of his mouth. He breathes deeply the fresh morning air. Finally, he speaks. *This is the best apple I have ever tasted, I swear it.* Sweeter than the Braeburns from the grocery store; crisper even than all the varieties growing in his orchard at home, the place he left behind so many miles from here.

This morning he will make a memory of this apple. He begins to color this moment, (she can see him doing it), with such smooth edges, such richness of detail, giving it a fragrance deeper than any apple could possibly have. He will make its sugared juice and crisp bite finer than any apple ever grown on any tree on earth. An apple that could only grow in Paradise. He does not offer her a bite, does not ask what she thinks of the apple's flavor. He does not want anything that might diminish his belief.

No apple in the harsh light of a different day, one not tasted this very morning behind this old hotel, here at the patio table in this light with this woman, will ever be able to compare to the thing he has made of it. *There will never be another apple as good as this one,* he says, not knowing the weight of his own words, how he has condemned himself to a life of lesser apples. But it is what he must do, his one hedge against loss: the only thing he can take with him from a day he cannot keep.

BOY PRUNING ROSES

The tanned and handsome youth in shorts and work boots
is here again in the Museum Gardens with his shears.

In the low afternoon light, he steps carefully into the rows
of white roses. Bush after bush of blossoms thrive,

an abundance of petals, a whole world of multi-layered pearl.
His large hands delicately lift each thin stem.

He studies each individual rose.
Then, without hesitation, he snips off the bloom.

Creamy white flowers, some at the height of their opening,
he cuts off and tosses into a rusty green wheelbarrow.

From my blanket on the grass, I watch as they pile up.
I feel my old need to hoard, the panic of loss.

The boy shrugs. "Help yourself," he says, although
he doesn't understand why I'm digging through the castoffs.

Then holding a rose in his young hand, he tells me,
"You know, the more they are cut, the more they will bloom."

The browning blossoms droop in my hands, while on the bushes
tight buds are poised to open, some maybe tomorrow.

And I will carry the dead roses home, evidence of how I live
in scarcity, the forgotten plenty of the world.

TELEPHONE TREE

It is early when we get that call,
the message over a bit of static,
passed from neighbor to neighbor along a chain.

No one has a clue how it could have
happened, this young life extinguished
too early, taken by his own hands.

There is talk of the gun: where did he get it?
In his parents' yard, one shot, muffled
in moonlight, out back by the lilac bushes.

Horror races toward us, unprotected in our
sunny kitchens. We can see the blood spilled
as if on our own green lawns, the tender skin

of children's faces split open, eyes wide and
blank. We cringe in its too easy possibility
and, shaking, hang up the phone.

We have learned by now how to handle
this kind of thing, the rules we've agreed to
that save us from panic.

Each mother takes a job we can do
to get us through the days, keep
moving, not think too much.

A schedule is arranged to bring food,
large quantities, casseroles and quick breads,
dishes that will easily freeze.

Friends offer their hands to the grieving parents,
the fiancée who stops counting
the days until their wedding.

The morning they bury their son, we say all our
practiced words, useless but reliable,
that pretend to comfort, at least until the night.

It is there in the silent dark
of our own rooms that it arrives, finally,
what we have refused to look at,

the terror that passes behind our eyes,
that shadows the light of our distant suns.
It comes and goes like regular trains.

The boy who shot himself after only 27 years
is not flawed in some elaborate way.
Sorrows abound, immeasurable, ordinary.

Tonight after we've all hung up the phones,
we'll go down the hall in the dark
to check on our own sleeping children.

Certain of our powerlessness,
we'll pull up the covers under their chins,
and look a long time at their faces.

SURRENDER

As if the undersides of leaves flicking against blue
tugged in autumn's late wind were fish and the fish silver
wriggling to be released into a stream, into silver
water racing over pebbles left behind by glacier's
sifting hands, as if the water's stream was hands, silver
skin sliding across burnished rocks sleek with time,
as if time were silver drops skimming along skin
running down its surface to unknown depths, as if
the silver skin is a woman's, her fingers the fingers of water,
swimming in ancient, perpetual streams, permeable,
her skin dissolving to silver water, transparent, freed now
from skin and edges, slipping like time across silver
surfaces flowing to immensity of sea, as if the surface
seals above her like glass reflecting blue sky where
the undersides of leaves tug like fish wanting release.

BREVITY

If you hear the wind rattle
the loose window glass,
or the squirrel's small paws
tramping along the roofline,
you may find that it is only
your restless self, longing
to cross the border.
All at once you see how
one day you'll quietly slip out
of your life like that.
Quick as the scent of fresh sawdust,
the color of your childhood room,
the monarch touching its thread feet
to the milkweed—a pulse of orange
and it lifts off into summer air.

THINGS I'D TELL YOU IF I KNEW HOW
TO REACH YOU

About these dreams I've been having lately where I crash my car, scrape the
chrome against hard things, scratch off paint, dent the metal, and me
at fault, always.

And this urgency under my skin, electric charges misfiring as if
synapse sparks are badly timed, random leaps from neuron to neuron
across too-wide spaces.

This unexpected February fog, all wrong. Clouds should be frozen, not hungrily
moving; the way they suck white snow away and spit back grime.

You know how I look through windows all day, a bad habit.
The glass is smudged with the residue of old rain and fingerprints.

How fragments of memory poke me like spikes: buildings I don't recognize
but believe I should know, steep rocky hills unlike my real landscape,
streets I can't recall walking.

The news anchorwoman is wound up too fast, a robot gone berserk;
her words bang my head too loud. What she says seems important,
crucial gibberish I can't decipher.

That everything is bigger than the person who watches it. What I record
is only a fragment of what it is, a pale snapshot from one angle,
full view unobtainable.

How I planted so many bulbs last fall: crocus, daffodils, a frenzy of faith,
but I am afraid they won't come up in spring. Or I'm afraid they might,
and I'll be responsible for them.

TRAIN RIDE

Now low hills of grass the color of sand,
yellow-tan, a scattering of dark cows,
a horse, then two, gray ice holding on
to a pond near the tracks. Sand-colored
brush spreads all directions. Makes me want
to breathe deeper. On the loudspeaker:
Set your clocks back as we go through
Williston, North Dakota, to a new zone.
A single duck flaps, frantic, works to
gain altitude over a wet field, pumps hard,
all muscle, no glide, lacks elegance
but makes up for it in effort. An honest
Midwestern bird. I can imagine
the miles he must cover and how weary,
at the end of the day, he'll be, how he'll
settle at last on a chill puddle at the edge
of a stubble field. Now a semi truck
pulls a huge tank, climbs a winding road
into sand-colored hills, raises a spray
of yellow dust in a path behind.
It grows smaller and smaller, the truck
now a toy, then a blur, dissolves into
a sand-colored cloud, then dissipates
to nothing, the scruffy hill it climbed
left as still as it began. As I roll forward
time telescopes and what I did
in my former life just yesterday
has no substance; all is now, this
looking out the window, everything
steadily moving backward but I
slice straight into it, my words unnecessary
bright flags flapping out the back door
in the wind. They begin to shred, diffuse
into the vast, wide shape of the space
I ride through, surrounded on all sides
and into infinity of sky by rolling light.
I give up time in favor of distance.

It spreads, unbroken. At my window
a flash of light, unidentifiable,
a possible streak of what's still to come.
The muted train whistle sounds again
and I, too, vanish.

AS I SMELL THE FIRST LEAVES OF AUTUMN, I THINK OF AN OLD FRIEND

It arrives as reliable as a birthday, this ritual
that rides in on drafts of chill air, that accompanies
the russet, yellow, reddening of the trees along
the boulevard. The breeze carries a scent
from childhood, when I would crunch dry leaves
under my shoes as I zigzagged slowly
to school. Today again the wind's bony hands
deliver the essence of decay, inevitable
crushed summer, long-gone suppleness drained
to brown. Like that long-ago time when
you and I strolled toward the station,
reluctant to arrive. Your bag was light;
you hadn't meant to stay long. Was it morning
that last day, the light long and slanting
through branches, dappling us with gold? Or did I
put the sun there later, painter of my own history?
Memory is an undependable friend. I know this much:
the noise of fallen leaves under our feet
was the only sound. And the train was on time.

A sound like today, many years after,
as I collect leaves, choosing one at a time, beautiful
colors I can't keep. I press them
in heavy books, even a dictionary,
in honor of you, who loved words sometimes
more than the real things they stand for.
When I open the pages weeks from now,
I will find them again, crumbled
to dust. Still, I keep collecting.

CLUES

All the train poems
Are about one train.

The universe hands you a ticket
With nothing written on it.
You get to choose whether
You'll board, going east or west,
Or not.

Meanwhile the seasons
Keep cycling through
Their frustratingly
Comfortingly
Predictable patterns.

Motion remains constant
So it's hard to tell
Where the still point might be
(If there is one)
In all that turning.

You begin to notice:
Everything that flies—
Insects, birds, wishes, desire—
Must rest somewhere at last.

What should have been obvious
Knocks on your door.
Even your daughter
Will find a gray hair
One day, too,
And eventually you end up
In the place where you are.

OPERA WORKSHOP REHEARSAL

Walking the cobbled streets of Spoleto, we heard music
drifting out from within an old church. Italian opera arias,
rising powerful, unfamiliar to our ears, drew us close.

Curious, we wandered inside, sat on a pew in the back.
Under the vaulted ceiling, dim glow of a summer day
filtered through the glass. Young men and women

one by one stood, took deep breaths and sang out
solos, each voice a soaring surprise, conjuring
the burst of a single bird through a boundless sky,

melodies rising like a million morning suns.
Each voice controlled a galaxy, the breath lifting,
carrying, holding aloft and then releasing each note,

singularly exultant, to the wide world. Though many
were shaking as they stepped forward for their turns,
their young, strong voices launched fearlessly

into what they had been training for years to do,
like elite athletes, but with song instead of javelin,
hurling the expression of creation forward, beyond

their youth, past their teachers coaching from the aisles,
larger than any individual, until it rose
to the peak of that ceiling, up near the gilded trim,

up into the steeple, escaping through open windows,
swelling like waves, surges of sound shaped into form,
and you and I, on a break from our writing class, stumbled

into that unexpected heaven, sat cautiously, still,
afraid of breaking the spell. I entered the atmosphere of sound
unaware of how it would grab me, wrap around my skin,

saturate my cells until I was drinking the music.
How it filled me like the richest wine, until tears rose,
streamed down my face, the closest thing to tangible awe

until you whispered that you were ready to leave,
abruptly shattering my reverie. I was ashamed then
of how my heart had risen on invisible winged notes,

become exposed. Instead of telling you *No*, how I wanted
to stay as long as I could in that rare atmosphere,
I hurried to hide my opened self, followed you out.

You did not look back. But I did, to get a last glimpse
of a young woman trembling on the steps up front
after lifting her song, visibly spent, glowing with pride.

And then I stepped out into the bright Spoleto day
with nowhere to go, already bereft from the loss
of that song, knowing I would never be there again,
walking away from what might have saved me.

AFTER READING GEORGE'S ACCOUNT
OF OUR TIME TOGETHER IN SPOLETO

I'll admit it: memory
is an independent artist.

Taking fragments of the real
as its pigments, it crushes them,

time's lapis lazuli, red ochre, malachite,
mixes them with its own oils,

formulating its favorite colors.
On the canvas of the mind

it asserts creative license,
swirls broad swaths

inspired by images from its past
but always insistent on reconstruction.

Like the ancient aqueduct we stood on
overlooking the deep valley, as the bells

from the stone church rang,
bringing down the Italian evening sun.

Today, many years after, you describe
your version, painted in sweeping hues,

grand strokes of Hannibal's elephants,
historical allusions, and I barely recognize

the place. Mine is about sweat,
the hike up the hill to get there,

the touch of your skin,
my own red beating heart,

the single summerwhite butterfly
that played among the weeds.

WHERE LOVE RESIDES

They fall into exhaustion rather than into gentle sleep,
    each limb heavy with the ash of its bonfires burned completely down,
        not curled but sprawled, claiming all the space of their bed,

Two bodies that attempted fusion. Both strained to push into
    what is impenetrable in the other, wanting in the only way they know
        to try, to perhaps break through the inherent loneliness of skin.

Now, very late, leg over leg, arm across chest, they breathe deep as newborns,
    as if drawing from the air replenishment after their struggle. No dreams
        tonight. Instead, only thick flesh, cooling back into their separate selves.

What will they say when they stir back into the world,
    conscious, suddenly, of their edges as morning sun floods their sheets?
        What will their first words be upon waking?

Each will arrive in the new day alone, surprised, as they were at their births,
    and at death, and as after each sleep, utterly bound in the locked rooms
        of their bodies. Will they recognize their loneliness? Will they
            speak of it?

If love resides anywhere, it is here: in the most fragile moment,
    the waking faces, their mussed hair. When habitual seeing returns.
        It is in their decision, whether or not they will
            tell one another of their true need.

STORIES TOLD DURING A LONG DRIVE

It's getting hot in the car, so I roll down my window, even though
the wind whips in and blows my hair around. I used to sleep outside,
I tell my husband, in a tent we pitched in the backyard in summer,
my best friends from the neighborhood and me. Our parents, indoors
with the noisy window air conditioner running, were oblivious while we
stayed awake long into the night, playing Truth Or Dare, talking about
the minister's son with the dreamy blue eyes, or the 16-year-old up
the road who always shot freethrows in his driveway with his shirt off.

My husband turns down the radio, an oldies station playing Steely Dan.
We'd climb out of the tent in the middle of the night, I say, and walk up
the black-top road, tar still hot from the day sticky on our bare feet. If a car
came, we'd jump into a grassy ditch, lie still until its headlights passed.
Then we'd climb over the fence into Koepsel's backyard to steal sour
green apples from their tree, not because we were hungry and not because
they tasted good—(every bite made my teeth itch and my mouth pucker)—
but just so we could prove we were bold. I tell him how we'd plan our
escape, running through the farmer's field, in case their hunting dogs
began to bark. It felt good to run like that, full speed back to the tent with
our hands and pockets full of small, hard apples.

My husband behind the wheel looks out across the cornfields, rows of green
flitting past almost too fast to see. Then he takes a handful of crunchy dried
wasabi peas we've brought for a snack, hands me the bag, and says, *Let's
turn off the highway, take the scenic route for a while.*

FOR NO APPARENT REASON

On a crisp, sunny Saturday, she was dead, the top
of her middle son's head in the back seat sliced off
by flying metal, her own face ripped by smashed glass,
everything soft split apart. There must have been time
only for a quick glance at her lover in the passenger seat,
a sudden realization, and then the impact. On the grassy
shoulder of the road out in the middle of nowhere, the
paramedics and cops were sloppy, left behind the contents
of her purse: a comb, a broken mirror, a ticket stub
from a concert and a child's plastic Transformer toy,
the kind you can twist and change from vehicle to superhero,
scattered among the sparkling splinters of glass.
The week before the accident, she had been oddly moved
to give flowers to strangers. Couldn't explain why, even to
the one best friend she had in that small town, but it was
a strong urging, so she went out and bought roses, pink ones,
an armful, walked down the street and gave them away without
a word. The usual stoic faces of the people along Division Street
must have looked astonished, but no one turns down a rose.

WHAT IF

(after Li-Young Lee)

What if when I say *song* I mean
the light that rises steadily above the trees
until dark dissolves to beginning,
but when you say *song* you mean
an ache made visible
in the white spaces of your room?

What if by *story* I mean
the path that leads into an October forest,
but you mean a sailboat on rough seas
over weeks and weeks?

And what if by *time* I mean
the invisible forward and backward
of a string with many knots,
but you mean
the horizon that can't be seen?

I roam my own body looking for landmarks
while you step out your door
in the middle of the night.
My dreams float me in a mist of bewilderment;
I hold binoculars to my eyes.
What is solid vanishes when you give it a name.
What remains in my hands
takes on many changing shapes. How
can I tell you this?

THREE

"...Breathe it in and you start to remember things you didn't know you'd forgotten."

—*Robin Wall Kimmerer,*
in Braiding Sweetgrass

WEATHERING

Fog
A veil of secrets: all that is not said,
or the thing you can't admit.

Drizzle
A grudging shrug from a former lover that only matters
when you remember how his face used to light up.

First Snow, December
Ease of sleep under feathers in a round, whitewashed room.
No shadows, no corners.

Blizzard
Blind buzzing of furious white bees
uncertain where home is.

Below-zero Sun
The bite of a tart lemon that makes you wince,
its icy juice sipped through the teeth.

Hoarfrost
The hands on your clock abruptly stop;
all that is brilliant reveals itself for only an instant—
then disappears. You can't prove it ever existed.

Thunder and Lightning
Blunt answers to the questions
you couldn't bear to ask out loud.

Humid Haze, 95 Degrees
Waiting for the object of your deepest desire.
Time stretches excruciatingly.

Cloudless Blue Sky
All the living things look up at once and sing a single clear note.

Steady Rain at Daybreak
Heaviness can no longer hold its shape,
dissolves into minuscule gray shards.
No promises made today.

Heavy Clouds Hiding Sun
Not joy, but the fear of it. Hesitation before entering what might be
exactly what you always wanted. Or not.

Rainbow
Pale echo of your heart's most private wish, suddenly made public,
pursued until you are drenched with hope and shame.

MY FATHER'S CLOSET

The boxes wait, big and empty,
for the clothes he won't be wearing any more.
The once-familiar creak of the sliding closet door
sounds too loud in the silent house.

When I was little, I'd sneak in here,
rummage behind the shoe racks,
his neckties hanging down
like vines in a dark woods.
I'd part them to glimpse hidden
Christmas presents. Sometimes I'd try on
his too-big shoes, stomp around him
as he tied his tie in front of the dresser mirror.
Or I'd sift through pieces of gift-wrap paper
and bows of every color,
arrange them in a rainbow on the big bed.
Today I've already pulled out everything from the back,
sorted it dispassionately, thrown stuff away,
the efficient, organized oldest daughter.

Now here are his suits,
lined up, stiff-shouldered, neatly pressed.
I'd never noticed how much gray he wore,
the sameness of the tweeds, steadfast and predictable.
I flip through the hangers, sliding three-piece suits,
his lawyer's uniforms, along the rack.
Evidence of my father slips out in bits:
wisps of old cigar smoke smell,
then a sudden spicy cologne scent I have always known.
A row of shirts, white and white and pale blue and white,
even one with a ballpoint pen still stuck in the pocket,
cling stubbornly to their hangers.
They begin to whisper to me, these shirts,
these navy and burgundy and gray-striped ties,
these suits—his unsentimental, unshakeable voice,
the kind of voice that always penetrates.
I hear the murmur of years, harsh
and tender, a confused cacophony.

I move slowly now, watching my own hands
as if they might be someone else's.
The feel of a gray padded shoulder
surprises my fingers with its warmth.
I lean into the closet.
When did I get tall enough
to put my face into his shoulder?
I rub my face on a limp sleeve,
close my eyes; the rough fabric
like the maleness of his unshaven face,
giving me a "beard rub" when I was six.
I lift the wide shoulders; the jacket slips off
into my arms, at last released.
I wrap myself around the lifeless form.
It crushes easily under my touch.
We sink into the closet's thick, gray shadows.

NOVEMBER WALK AROUND THE LAKE

This is the day you know will be the last
before the wind sweeps harsh
across the lake. The sky is milky-pearl,
the iridescent inside of a seashell.

You walk the familiar circular path past
retired couples arm in arm, a man with silver
hair jogging hard, panting, the young
women with their fouffy little dogs,
the families biking. Everyone's aware: this
is likely the last bright day we'll get.

The gold of November scatters about you,
illuminates beamed and brick houses.
Autumn's litter of dry brown crumbs settled
on the path's edge seems not yet sad.
You lengthen your stride. Memories
that have almost slipped begin to stir

as the chill nips your ears and you round
the far end. You are plunged into the dark half
of the circle-path where no sunlight touches.
Cold knocks at your bones; you pick up your pace,
feel your hamstring muscles pull. Then you realize
all at once you can't remember what he looks like.

You have already lost the details: the exact shade of blue
of his eyes, the size of his hands. He comes to you
in shards—a fringe of black hair, a raised eyebrow.
He is an idea instead of a man. This side of the lake
is lonely; you hurry to get around. The path is circular;
it will surely bring you back to light.

You walk faster, but when you reach the other side,
it's not at all the place where you began.
You have forgotten so much of what you loved.
The light is low like a dying fire; the cold is grabbing hold.

An elderly couple rests on a bench. Their skin glows pink.
You think of that old aching Sinatra song *Someone*
To Watch Over Me. They sit far apart;
both look out toward the lake, no longer blue.
Even these words you are thinking will be gone
before you get home and can write them down right.

VIEW FROM THE SEATS

We are long tamed. We settle in, faces
all turned in one direction, waiting.
There was a rumor that something will happen
so we have come, single-file, and sit politely.
No raised arms, only whispers into the dark;
we hold still within the careful edges.
The woods at the borders tremble slightly
but the stage is well-lit and whatever wildness
is coming will be confined to that distant box.

We would wait here all night. We breathe
almost in unison, quietly, anonymous bodies
unidentifiable singly but together comprising
a mass. We are happy with our invisibility.
Watching is so much neater; the armchairs
hold us snugly. Our attention poised meekly
forward on the place where love is bigger
than death, where unsayable tragedy may be made
bearable. Where one cannot be trapped forever

in a winter of discontent or a swollen pool
of desire. The mad ones might spin down
into their own dissolving reflections but can't
pull anyone in with them. Yet we did
venture out with strangers on a night
when we could have stayed in our beds.
We know we risk the press of awe,
the smells of passion wafting out at us.
Voices will surely ring out and it may get loud.

The agonizing and the beautiful: everything will be
included, one evening as a lifetime. We could not
live this way, with crystal hearts, walking through
the doors of the underworld. We could not carry
the heavy bottles of wine, the thorned roses.
Instead we gather as cautious witnesses.
We will clap at the end, zip our jackets
and file out neatly to our cars, almost satisfied.

STORIES TOLD WHILE WALKING AROUND THE LAKE

I went through a climbing phase, her husband tells her, as they step onto the trail on a breezy spring evening. Maybe every teenage boy does, when his strongest desire is to ascend any tall, forbidding structure: a roof, a bridge, the water tower—just for the exhilaration of getting up above everyone. One night at midnight, he confides, he snuck out of the house with a three-pronged grappling hook he made in shop class, attached to a knotted rope. From the sidewalk at the base of the power plant, he threw the hook up until it caught, then climbed hand over hand to the smokestack ladder, two stories up. He climbed that ladder to the very top of the smokestack, then looked out across his small Minnesota town from the highest point. He remembers it was warm that night, and oddly peaceful up there.

Just then, in the dark, he says, a friend from high school pulled up on his motorcycle, stopped at a stop sign on the street directly below and, for some unknown reason, turned off his engine. He yelled down, "Dave! Dave!" and his friend looked this way and that for where the voice was coming from. How strange to be so high above, invisible, until at last his friend spotted him improbably on the top of the ladder on the town's tallest smokestack.

She takes her husband's hand as they walk the familiar path around the lake. *My mother never knew I did that,* he says, looking out across the calm water. *Dave was the only witness.* And now she knows, too.

GATHERING STONES ON THE BEACH

Deception Pass, Washington

You peruse the thousands of stones arrayed
on this cold bleached afternoon:
Their ancient composition, minerals

derived from deep in the earth,
shined for a moment by licks of saltwater.
Which ones to take? As the afternoon grows long,

you choose carefully: one for its pearly sheen,
maybe a reddish speckle, the jet black stripes,
or a vein of quartz clear as ocean water.

They dry, grow dull again in the hand,
their stories hard to discern.
History compressed. What is left after

the mountain has been weathered away.
Time itself, in tightly-packed containers,
all their elements inextricable,

as ours are. Nothing can be pulled away,
even as we are tumbled, scoured.
You scan the rocks again; you love them all,

not for their shine, which has worn off,
but for the smooth way they turn and turn
against each other in the palm, clattering

a whispery, clickety sound,
speaking what they remember
of the planet's long biography.

ON THE DISCOVERY OF A BASILOSAURUS
SKELETON IN THE WADI HITAN DESERT

They've unearthed the bones at last, elegant proof
of how whales once walked the earth, then made a u-turn
back to the call of the sea. Here in this desert-once-ocean,
the in-between being offers two delicate hind legs
to the reverent hands of the paleontologist.
Useless for walking, eight inches long, thin
as a child's thighs, these limbs link landcrawlers
with the great water-borne creatures.

From tetrapod,
salamander slim, that hauled itself onto muddy shore
360 million years ago, the mammals came.
Fins to legs, lungs for breathing air, they filled
the earth. But now we know:

a gradual return.
What siren sang them back to sea?
Rejecting terrestrial plans, they longed only
to swim again, to eat the ocean's bounty, mate in its
watery hold, move with the ease they remembered.
So they worked a backwards spell:

transformed feet
back into flippers. The bones still hold the history.
Tails flatten to flukes, eyes migrate sideways,
nostrils move up, rise and spout over millennia.
They must have preferred aquatic life, happy
to dive and breach, skim through blue deep,
their weight morphed into power.
What strength of will to give up dry land,
to change their very selves through sustained desire.

SPEAKING IN TONGUES

"I don't know
with what tongue
to answer
this world's constant question..."
    —Jane Hirshfield, "A Breakable Spell"

I could answer
with the tongue of early sunlight
that slants sideways through the window,
or the tongue of street sweeper that brushes
the curb, or of the boy who bicycles
to school sleepily. His wheels
on the road make a sound
like the hiss of cool water on a hot pan.
Or the tongue of shy things:
the jumping spider climbing the wall,
the cat that rubs my ankles.
It's a wonder that anyone hears
the question at all. The world requires
quiet attention, beneath the noise
of airplanes, traffic's constant growl.
I propose hesitant responses.
I try *crow, grass, day lily;*
all hold their moments
of yes, then gone.
I try the larger wonders,
the ones I don't comprehend:
mountain, heart.
It keeps asking.
Perhaps it's not an answer
the world wants. Maybe
just some exchange
as I make the coffee,
the tongue of the grinder releasing
the beans' dark essence
before the phone rings.

SCOURING NIKUMARORO

"Never interrupt someone doing what you said couldn't be done."
—Amelia Earhart

Every tiny fragment found makes their hearts spin.
They've been here before, following the last
signals, compass numbers, lost bones, hope
for touch DNA from bits of a knife blade.

They've sought the truth since 1937, these scholars
and obsessives, traced the aviatrix to this place:
southeast end of a remote Pacific island
where doubters swear the Electra crashed and sank.

Dense scaevola frutescens guards the site,
a perfect hiding place for human bones
perhaps carried away by giant coconut crabs
after they demolished all of her remains.

Could she have landed on the fringing reef?
It's surely flat enough at low tide.
A last distress call mentions rising water.
A hero doesn't crash; she holds out to the end.

Convinced Amelia and Fred were survivors,
castaways, (their ring of fire scar, remnants of a shoe,
that pocket knife blade beaten apart),
these seekers tell the story no one can quite prove.

Her mystique, grown larger in disappearance,
calls them even now to speculate, conduct pig bone
experiments, send an underwater probe
over a thousand feet down the reef's slope.

After her first barnstormer airplane ride,
Amelia said, "As soon as I left the ground, I knew
I myself had to fly." And their continuing quest, too,
compels them, inexplicable and true.

DOG RUNNING WITH HIS MAN

For the sleek golden retriever, it is relief,
this bounding along the shore with his man.
Most of the time, it is all he can do to keep
his nerves within his skin, being assaulted
as he is every second of his life with
gorgeous smells, a constant heady flooding
from the world. It rushes at his too-keen nose:
sea salt, dead fish, rich green weeds
left behind by fingers of tide.
So much! The tingling edges of pine forest,
urines sprayed on every tree, sweet
sting of dung, bird tracks and tracks of other dogs
pressed lightly in wet sand, a bit of salami
to the left, dropped from a picnic, faint wood smoke
from a distant bonfire, and oh, the high he gets
from a whiff of female canine musk. Impossible
to know what to do with such happiness,
what he perpetually wants but can barely bear.
How it propels his fast, muscled flanks,
makes his ribs heave, his tongue pant.

At the end of the run, the man bends down,
offers a *good boy,* pats the young dog, his simple
loyal companion, never knowing
all that he carries, all that he craves.

CATALOGING HOLINESS

Some mornings I wake up astonished.

Gold at the window, a thousand shades of green
along the backyard path. Hissing cicada hum,
scent of grasses and wild sage.
Some small furred creature darts
behind a bush. All ordinary, but that day
imbued with a particular light,
their essences distilled, made visible.

There is a joy born of such abundant light,
the kind that pours into the morning,
rising as if it's a lustrous liquid filling
a glass jar. I walk out among the waking
insects, the stretching stalks, wafting
wet sweetness of soil, early shoots pushing
through barely-warm ground, bejeweled with dew.

I do not know the names of these young blooms.
I do not need to know. I'd rather study
their forms at my feet, smell and touch them
gently with my own hands. I meet them
as friends; we don't need a proper introduction.
Discovery is more delicious than knowledge.
I gather sensations and carry them gladly with me.

Entering the silence of my familiar woods
I am hushed, calmed. Trees rise in self-assured
solidness, and my gaze rises with them.
Do they know I am taking notes?
Can they sense my keen attention to their shapes,
their curves and angles? How do they feel
about being watched like this?

They go about their business, perhaps
indifferent. Just in case, I give them a friendly greeting.
My heart is fond of each one, separately,
and yet is also devoted to the whole, the way
it is woven together into a larger tapestry,
strands of forest color and scent entwining to
complete the design. Not only the tranquility,

but also the terrible power: the red tail hawk
poised on a limb, patient hunter of the unsuspecting,
its deep hunger, the inevitability of pursuit,
capture, desperation, fight and eventual surrender,
the everyday dramas of those who must kill to live.
This, too, I collect, one more expression
of a truth—the ferocious will to survive.

And the unseen, whose existence I take on faith:
the echoing knock of beak against bark,
the flash of black wing out of the corner of my eye,
the swift disappearances of squirrel or snake
before I can fix them in recognition, the invisible
wind, whose powerful hands can push
from out of nowhere with surprising insistence.

Farther on, the lapping water on the lake
burbles, ripples, splishes softly
as it touches shore. Listen to the language
the lake is speaking. I cannot translate it.
Even though it is foreign, I delight in the melody,
the lilting vowels and how it rises
at the end of its sentences. I do not exaggerate.

Silvered water bounces light back
to my eyes: glint of sun now too bright
to look at directly, white shine where
all color has fled, the doubled willow leaning
over the surface. All important ideas
are expressed in these things. Water embodies
constant change, the ever-turning and returning.

What right do I have to speak for
the sacred things of this world? No,
I cannot know what it is that they want to say.
I can only watch and listen, point to them,
collect, list, describe so that we might notice.
Such sheer abundance is not for our benefit;
It has no need of our admiration.

In the human darkness of our time,
it is easy to forget all that is holy.
A book of a billion billion pages
could not contain it. A lifetime of extraordinary length
will never be enough. But I am compelled
in the hours and days I have left
to keep cataloging the elements,

unafraid to be excessive,
as nature herself is excessive.

WHAT COUNTS

At ten p.m. you wandered upside the inside of my head
you caught me singing—I resisted but you could hear
what was spilling & you told me about something you read
maybe in National Geographic about what makes people happy
statistically—a religious affiliation social connections
financial security stable home environment it all depends
& you asked me *How happy are you? On a scale of 1 to 10*
I hummed hawed fidgeted wondered what counts as happy
the small unstatistical things—it doesn't take much at least
for some of us—depends on if you've got the mountain
or the valley view & do you like the view out your own window
whether you're driving or in the passenger seat—can you choose
can you sing in a tunnel—can you stand your own reverberations
& how long must you stay & if you decided to be here or
if you were pushed   *A 9*, I finally say, *I am a 9*
& you are surprised *But that means it's almost perfect*
I nod go back to my song don't ask but you tell me anyway
I'd say I'm at about a 7   Do I have to wonder what is missing?
because a 9 would be certain that you'll find it eventually &
if we can successfully ignore time there's no need to rush
& here is as good as there

THEORY OF SONG

In snowthick woods
a swarm of children plays,
clambering over logs,

rocks, hilldrifts of white,
a scurry of bodies
bundled thickly

in puffy snowsuits, bright
pink, turquoise, swathed
in woolen scarves, hats,

their eyes and noses
the only human features.
Frenzy of motion up, down

like determined squirrels,
they wrestle the mounds,
sink into snowpiles

and, from a distance,
their squeals and calls
merge into a joydriven,
high-pitched hum.

No individual voices,
no words left
in their flurried noises.

How the melody rises
when a boot gets stuck,
how it crescendoes
when one slides down a slope,

bodies plunging into the world
with an ease so deep
their sounds ascend beyond language:
the origins of music.

FOUR

"...Our lives are small things,
easy to miss. The truth is
they do not belong to us at all,
but must, in the end, be returned to the sky..."

—Jim Moore,
from his poem "The Long Experience of Love"

VIEW AT FIFTY-FIVE

(after Jim Moore)

1. The snow is part of it, gentle and inevitable,
How it settles over every rough surface.
And perhaps the last streaks of sun at dusk.
What used to be rushed is calmer now.
I breathe in the subtle colors
Of sky, water, winter-bare trees,
Perceive their infinite shades of difference,
Something I failed to see
When I was younger
And so much in a hurry
To accomplish all the items on my scrawled lists.
I pour a glass of red wine,
Answer your question about how my writing is going
With a small smile, a sigh
And look out the window again.

2. How it settles over every rough surface.
I breathe in the subtle colors,
Something I failed to see
On my scrawled lists.
I pour a glass of red wine
With a small smile, a sigh
And look out the window again.

3. Perhaps the last streaks of sun at dusk,
Infinite shades of difference,
Answer your question
With a small sigh.

4. Something I failed to see
When I was so much in a hurry,
How it is going—

5. I look out the window again.

PORTRAIT OF A JANUARY MORNING
IN BLACK AND WHITE

The neighborhood asleep. Thin dust of snow
Whitely muffles sidewalks. From branches overhead,
Silence shatters: raucous caws of crows.

They dot crocheted branches black as ink
 Like small knots tied in a veil of black lace.
Then they rise up, a gust of dark wind, in sync.
A flustered rush, sudden scattering, they take
Flight, as if some great invisible hand had tossed
Confetti through the air to startle me awake.

Those crows, as they crisscross paths, dart by,
Slash sharp above stark trees, leave me below
Awed by glass wings crosshatching white sky.
At once: bodies and cries so sharp they pierce
The cold, and I who watch can only admire
Anything that bears a calling so fierce.

Then they settle again on bare branches and still,
As if they had never been stirred at all.
And I, too, wide awake, sense the calm in the chill.

IT'S NOT TIME

At sixteen I wore a pale yellow polyester top,
easy to launder, and soft-soled white shoes,
a pin-on name tag. Each afternoon after school
when I walked through the nursing home doors,
that familiar smell grabbed me: wilted flowers,
soiled sheets, bleach, something vaguely beefy
that had been cooking a long time. Metal carts
shelved sharp-folded white linens. The moaning lady
waited for a bus in the hallway outside her room,
perpetually wondering why it was late.
The white-haired women who still wore
lipstick called me *Dear*. My job was simple.
I brought up trays of dinner from the kitchen,
domed bowls of purees, brown, greenish, orange,
or soft meatloaf, mashed potatoes, Jello. I spooned
it into the mouths of those who could not
do it themselves. I changed beds, made crisp edges,
tucked corners in tight. Listened to the talkers,
talked to those who had no more words.
In the smoking lounge, I lined up wheelchairs,
passed out cigarettes, lit them up for residents
(not allowed to keep lighters) while the TV,
always on loud, blared "The Price is Right."
They were already so old, no one worried about
the health effects; no one there was ever going to quit.
We were supposed to use Reality Therapy, tell
the gray man searching for his cap, *No, Henry, it's not time*
to go to the Brewers game, you're at Bethesda, you live here,
remember? it's almost time for your juice and crackers,
sit back down, no one's coming today to pick you up
to take you to the game, no one will be coming.

MY HUSBAND TELLS ME OF HIS DREAMS

His dreams lately are all about building:
he must erect scaffolding, and quickly,

a complex set of brackets, clamps and tubes
he must decipher and make sturdy;

or, as morning speeds toward him,
he understands he must reconstruct

a complicated machine in a tiny corner,
make the gears mesh and the rotors spin.

At breakfast he tells me of these nighttime tasks,
the sense of urgency involved,

as if something terrible will happen
if he can't complete the job in time.

The circumstances change each night
but the burden is the same: fix it,

or you will be responsible for tragedy.
So much is beyond our control. We listen

to the news on the radio, distant voices
relating factual horrors as we sit warm

and well-fed and helpless to affect anything.
Outside the dining room window, a full moon

caught in the branches of our crab tree
fades as the sky lightens with day.

It looks so close, we almost believe
we could climb up his tall ladder and touch it.

Illusions are everywhere. Later today the cardinal
will return, sit on his branch in that tree,

deep red like the berries that stay all winter,
a saturated flare against the white of snow.

We know the bloom will come again,
pink blossoms out that window, and green

leaves, and grass under the grimy melt.
But this morning, it is hard to remember.

We've come to recognize the cardinal's call,
alarming at first, until it became familiar.

Now the sound makes us glad. We know
that fellow, his mate likely nearby.

We don't know where the nest is, or why
he keeps coming back, or how he stands the cold.

Does our cardinal dream, too? Does he fret
with thoughts of urgent chores that must be done,

or chaos will ensue? We will watch him flit off
to who knows where. We eat our toast,

go throw a load of laundry into the machine,
turn off the radio voices. We trust spring,

but it won't come today. Not yet.

WHAT THE LAKE KNOWS

"In nature, the answers are always changing."
—Tom Hennen

Walking with my longtime friend in the last
days of winter, we lament the recent
turns of events, how hatred has bubbled up
as if from underground, spilling onto
the earth, winding its way in spreading
torrents across our feet, the terror
of its rising, rising above our ankles.

The unnatural swell of constant bad news
batters like stirred-up stormtide the borders of
our minds and hearts, our skin, and though
we try to stay alert, unguarded, we both admit
we're hardening, starting to wall-off the waves
of voices: the hurt, the ignored, the betrayed,
to try to protect ourselves from the surge.

Quiet now, we walk the path around the lake
that is still holding onto a sheen of ice;
who knows what stirs beneath its surface.
All at once the ice on the lake
thunders, rumbling surprising booms,
easy to mistake for distant traffic noise
unless someone lets you in on the secret.

My friend stops me. We listen together.
She is a woman of the north woods
and knows the language of the lake
as it shudders under its frozen layer,
beginning to shrug off its winter weight.
I can hardly believe my beloved water
speaks with such a guttural voice.

I have only heard its whispers, its summer
gentle song, the pulse of small waves.
This groan is so much deeper, with
startling power I've never realized.
Change is coming, it rumbles
with the wisdom of one who has witnessed
all of this many times before,

as it stirs with the patient knowledge
of inevitable thaw.

MY FATHER VISITS

The doorbell rings and he's standing on my front stoop
though he's been dead for more than a year.

Same thinning hair, dark-rimmed glasses, maybe a bit
shorter, and with an unfamiliar softness to his face,

his usual look of disapproval dissolved, as if it had been
erased by time or space. Somehow, I am not surprised.

I open the door, invite him to step inside my house,
the one he never wanted to visit. I politely offer him

a cup of tea, though I know he'll decline. I recognize
the smell of Old Spice, my favorite childhood scent.

I can't stay long, he says, and this makes sense to me;
there's somewhere else he's supposed to be.

Why is he here now? I'm wondering. Is this
a haunting? A reckoning? A wish?

As if he can read my thoughts, he says, *I just came
to see the baby.* My daughter, conceived too late

for him to meet when he was alive. I bring her in
from her crib. He reaches out his arms, wanting

to hold her, though I am hesitant. Can I trust
his appearance? I breathe deeply, hand her over.

All at once, he looks as if he has aged backwards,
become the young man he once must have been,

the father in my childhood photographs, before
I grew out of the sphere of his shine.

With a gentle hand, he lifts the baby's blanket,
gazes at her sleeping face. The words he says

are words I have never heard
my father say to anyone: *She is perfect.*

He hands me back the baby, turns and walks
out my door. I will never see him again, but

I will always know
that he showed up.

WHAT THE LAKE DOES TO YOU

Think back
to what's unreachable now,
maybe run aground on the far
beach, that once floated
within your arm's length, how water
never stops moving, even on a still
summer's day.

Listen
for sounds washed from the opposite
shore, echoing here, as if they could be
collected like smooth stones,
stacked into cairns for the heart to follow.

Consider the light
that ricochets in a million small sparks
until it blinds you, momentarily,
yet you continue to look.
How you can't take your eyes away.

Even when you walk along the shore
for miles, you never reach
what you've come for; it keeps drifting
away and your feet need the solid ground.

Bend down to put your hands in, slipped
between the silver coins, into cold
gray curtains, yards and yards of them,
folds that envelop you
until your hands grow numb, disappear
from the ends of your arms
and you can't bear to pull them out
to see what might be left.

STORIES TOLD WHILE WAITING FOR A PLANE

When I was thirteen, I tell my husband as we sit in the vinyl chairs
at the Gate 23 waiting area, my friend Linda and I would walk the path
through the corn field behind her house and sit under a big oak tree.
No one could see us from their windows. Linda would bring a swiped
pack of her mom's menthol Kools and a lighter. Long summer afternoons
she'd teach me how to hold a cigarette in a feminine way, between my
first finger and my middle finger, not the way the boys held theirs. I'd
draw in smoke, slowly pulling the heat from the lit end of Linda's cig
to light my own. One long drag after another in a continuous chain as
the day stretched out hot and slow in front of us.

The smoke that filled my lungs pulled against everything my parents thought
I was. I could finally breathe in the bigness of the world. The smoke made
me a little dizzy, as if I was floating just above the ground, as if I was rising
and falling through surging waves on a liquid, spinning planet. The haze and
the smell were what freedom was made of. I blew out expansive clouds, dreams
of who I might be, that dissipated above us. Then a voice over a scratchy
intercom calls our flight number, and my husband shoulders the strap of
his bag. We both love flying, letting the silver plane's incomprehensible
physics carry us to somewhere else. I hope this plane can slice through the fog,
my husband says as we walk single file with all the others down the jetway.

HIKING IN THE BLUE MOUNTAINS, NEW SOUTH WALES, AUSTRALIA

"What is description, after all,
but encoded desire?"
—Mark Doty

Hills of blue rise from valley floor:
dark indigo where I stand,
then sapphire blue; they roll to steel,

shift to azure smoke, then fade
in distant chiaroscuro haze.
Blue inside and outside of me—the blue of dreams

and memory merge with the blue of sky
and paler blue cloud as if
there is no beginning or end.

I breathe in this pause of soft
edgeless color, morning mist diffusing it
already into the shadows of its own brevity.

I love the language of the moment's
million attributes playing in the haze at once.
Water of melted snows here at my feet,

I need to tell of the trickle, the slide,
how it's glazed with sun, how it slips
down the ancient rock face

then is caught by the ledge below,
the swirl, the constant gurgled motion,
how water pools, then twists a path,

winds between rocks. I watch
water weave a braid of white,
thread its strands as with rapid hands,

wrap in and around, build to a rush,
gather its speed, then leap over the edge.
I watch the cascade plunge,

spray mist into gray-blue light,
fine drops blown back onto the trail.
How I long to inhale this exact day,

the spray on my skin that is cool and wet,
to transform it into something I can carry
with me through time, as if desire alone

was enough to perform an alchemy,
changing this instant of life through words,
to hold what is already slipping away.

As the falling water rubs against
that mountain shape and carves,
over time, the changing face,

how it indelibly imprints its course,
how rock always responds,
that's how I long to be reshaped.

Then I hike farther into the valley,
a damp trail, through dense eucalypt woods
and come suddenly into a kind of song:

some sort of Australian frogs, their call exactly like
the sound of clinking glasses. As if I had crossed
the threshold of a blue-green wonderland,

the sound crescendoes above and below me,
a thousand tiny creatures tapping their glasses
with tiny spoons as if calling for a bride and groom

to kiss, a merry tinkling sound of celebration.
I search in thick brush, on limbs of tree
and shrub, under wet leaves, on dark soil

but I can't see a single sign
of the animals whose call surrounds me
in every direction. All I can do

is stand still and listen
to the strange green music
of those invisible beings

in love, like me, with the wet
and blue-misted morning and later,
to try to gather that joy-filled music

into words, my futile but necessary
attempt to collect and preserve.
How sad I was

when their calls abruptly ceased
as I walked away from that glassy harmony.
I knew full well what would be lost.

If I say *the blue mist, the mountain waterfall,*
the frogs' clinking song, don't the words
begin to grasp a piece of that happiness,

even as I recognize how slippery its shape?
Doesn't it infuse in me, even a little bit,
that momentary heaven?

SATURDAY CANOE TRIP

It's all we can do now,
in the face of such noisy headlines,
to set the red canoe in the river
and, like the sleek muskrat,

muscle and glide with the current.
October sun rests low on top
of burnt boughs, rusty leaves
buoyed with the breeze.

There is a turtle
balanced on a log inches above
the water, sleeping in the sun as if
she's been there her whole life.

I don't know any answers,
and I've found that as my body
creaks and groans with the years,
nothing new is revealed.

I just grow more patient.
The sky's blue gets deeper, the sun
more fiery, leaves let go
and fall down faster.

I step off the shore in my boots
into the cold push of water,
glad for the solidness under my feet
as well as the quick flow.

We've packed our tent,
some nuts and dried fruit,
a box of macaroni and cheese
and, of course, some marshmallows.

I know there will be dead
wood for tonight's fire
and my beloved will be warm
next to me in our sleeping bag.

It's no answer
but it's a reason to continue
to breathe deeply and enter
this cold river, no need to go anywhere.

NOT LIKE THE GARDENS BACK HOME

Some landscapes spread out wide, invite
those of us who are stubborn learners,
who are perpetually skeptical and must
be shown again and again before we can concede
that something unfamiliar might be true.

Walking through this prairie, for instance:
its random messiness,
no human hand shaping or planting,
no arranging of short stems neatly in front
and taller ones behind; more like
a crowd than a choir. A brazen
black-eyed Susan pokes up
from amidst low clover—how it
delights in its unplanned way.
No gardener would have plunked
that lady among clumps
to rise like a showy diva. And
those milkweeds, thick, tough,
fuzzy green, next to delicate
Queen Anne's lace, accidental juxtaposition
that makes each of them more
of what they are.

I get down low, where gnats land
on the bare skin of my arms,
point my camera up through chewed leaves,
the green crochet of their flaws against sun.
Orange sherbet sky melts hot through the holes.
Bugs are sculptors, even as they also bite
my neck and hands. One fat bumblebee
flits among spiky purple flowers,
will not settle long enough
for my slow eye and hand
to catch it in focus, an apparition
I'll carry only in memory.

Things in this prairie defy capture.
They vanish in an exhale as if
the fact that they are so quickly gone
is part of their strange perfection.

GOING TO SEED

Halo of cloud,
stalk of slender green
bends in wind's pull,
surrenders to force without
moving its feet, holding
to summer as its white hair
loosens, flies free.

SUMMER ACCOUNTING

You count up everything you've been given
and what you can't have.
The sum is contentment and longing,
pushing and pulling at each other.

To the longing, you say:
There's a sliver of light at 8 p.m. that touches
the lifeguard chair across the silver beach,
shining the last mosquitoes and flickering
on dunegrass that waves in a darkening breeze.
A dead carp floats in the weeds, eyeless head
looking up toward the first star.

To the contentment, you say nothing.
June at the edges of things, turning
to July as you walk and walk.

LET ME BE A SPARROW

I'd like to be something a little less human,
    Not weighted with so many serious thoughts
        Here alone in a room without any windows.

To be something plain, not too complicated,
    Maybe one of these small brown birds
        That gather in the yard every afternoon.

Clustered in the cedars, on rosebush branches,
    They balance in breeze on high thin wires,
        Never one, or two, but many at once,

Ten or twelve or twenty or more
    Flutter down like a shower onto the grass.
        They peck and peck at what looks like nothing,

Frenetic hearts, speckled wings,
    Only as big as my open hand—
        I long to learn their trick of lightness.

They chatter and chirp in the dimming dusk
    And watch another summer unfold,
        As the raspberries ripen, the lilies open.

Nonstop, they comment with all of their passion,
    Whistle together to bring down the sun,
        Making bird-music of all they see.

What an honor it would be one day
    To be in such good company,
        Whose song outshines their brevity.

WHEN IT ENTERS

What if you woke one morning to find
you were permeable to birdsong?

You're walking the path through birch and oak;
it enters you at first the usual way.

A single note, then a trill, then more,
patterns repeat, a new voice joins,
an arpeggio. They weave under, over,

a pause; then higher, *whirr, ree,*
a long *caw* —You notice a tingle, your skin
lit up here, there, with sparks. Bits of song seep
through your pores, begin to fill each cell.

You, surprised, absorb it like raindrops
on parched ground. Into every empty
space their music pours. And still it comes!

You try to open, make room for
such audible force, continuous now.
Can you expand and expand
big enough to hold it all?

Or will you be like glass—a jar that fills
until it cannot hold one note more—
and crack? When the loon on the lake
cries her haunting grief, will you explode?

ACKNOWLEDGMENTS

I offer thanks to the editors of the following journals where these poems have been published previously, sometimes in earlier versions:

Awake in the World
Anthology of nature writing, Riverfeet Press
"Hiking in the Blue Mountains, New South Wales, Australia"

Beach Reads: Here Comes the Sun
Anthology from Third Street Writers
"New Love"

Beach Reads 3: Paradise
Anthology from Third Street Writers
"Not Like The Gardens Back Home"

Bearings (Collegeville Institute Newsletter)
"When It Enters"

Common Ground Review
"Portrait of a January Morning in Black and White"

Dog Blessings,
anthology edited by June Cotner,
New World Library
"Dog Running With His Man"

50/50: Anthology of Poetry by Women Over Fifty
Quill's Edge Press
"Summer Accounting"
"View At Fifty-Five"

Gyroscope Review
"What the Lake Knows"
"Things I'd Tell You If I Knew How To Reach You"

Helen: A Literary Magazine
"Let Me Be A Sparrow"

Iconoclast
"Brevity"

Into the Void
"My Father Visits"

Literati Quarterly
"Scouring Nikumaroro"
"Matrioshka"

Main Channel Voices
"African Violets"

Miramar Poetry Journal	"November Walk Around the Lake"
Nostos	"My Father's Closet"
	"Portrait With Lies"
Passager	"What The Lake Does To You"
(contest edition: Honorable Mention)	
Ponder Review	"It's Not Time"
The Sow's Ear Poetry Review	"Where Love Resides"
Spire Light	"Saturday Canoe Trip"
	"Aunty Fritz's Apartment"
Temenos	"Photo Negatives"
Third Wednesday	"Speaking in Tongues"
Trajectory	"Train Ride"
Welter	"What Counts"

The following poems appeared in the author's chapbook *I Have Always Wanted Lightning (Finishing Line Press, 2012)*: "Boy Pruning Roses," "Dog Running With His Man," "For No Apparent Reason," "Matrioshka," "Surrender," "The Apple," "Weathering" and "Where Love Resides."

Thank you to the members of my writing groups and dear friends who read many of these poems in their early stages and offered insight: Eileen Beha, Wendy Jerome, Amy Schwantes, Michael Gilligan, Deanna Lackaff, Lore Roethke, Al Wellnitz, Daryl Anderson, Dick Carlstrom, Joanna Reeves, and to Mary Jean Port for good advice. Deep gratitude also to my teachers in Hamline University's MFA program, especially Deborah Keenan, Jim Moore, Patricia Kirkpatrick and Barrie Jean Borich. For unconditional love and support, thank you to my husband Mike Hay, and to Pearl Devenow, who has been there with me through everything.

Joanne Esser has been writing poetry since she was a teenager, mostly to find out what she thinks, feels and knows. She got brave enough to begin sharing her writing with a few trusted writing groups when she was a young mother, eventually taking it more seriously and earning an MFA in Creative Writing from Hamline University. She was selected for the Mentor Series program at the Loft Literary Center in 2009 and published a chapbook of poems, *I Have Always Wanted Lightning*, in 2012 (Finishing Line Press). Many of her poems have been published in literary journals, including in *Welter, Temenos, Miramar, Gyroscope Review, Water~Stone Review, Passager, The Stillwater Review, Rock & Sling, Third Wednesday* and *Ponder Review*, among others. Her work has been included in the anthologies *50/50: Poems and Translations By Womxn Over Fifty (Quills Edge Press, 2018), Awake In The World*, an anthology of nature writing *(Riverfeet Press, 2017)* and *Dog Blessings*, edited by June Cotner *(New World Library, 2008)*. Joanne has also been a teacher of young children and/or a school administrator for over thirty years. As part of her practice, she writes a blog about her observations and reflections on children's learning. She lives in Minneapolis with her husband, Mike Hay. She has two grown daughters and a stepdaughter who are smart and beautiful, and four amazing grandchildren.